THE LILACS OF YEARNING

New and Selected Poems

Morton N. Felix

authorHOUSE®

AuthorHouse™
1663 Liberty Drive
Bloomington, IN 47403
www.authorhouse.com
Phone: 1-800-839-8640

First published by AuthorHouse 12/3/2010

ISBN: 978-1-4520-8064-2 (sc)

Printed in the United States of America

This book is printed on acid-free paper.

About the cover...The art work is a photograph by Barbara London of a pit-fired ceramic piece by Susan Duhan Felix called "The Lilacs of Yearning".

DEDICATION

To my dear wife:

My friend and loyal wife,

Who celebrates the moment
So time is always full,
And love replenished.

Thank you.

Vissi d'arte, vissi d'amore.

ACKNOWLEDGEMENTS

"A Poem for Peace" appeared in a December, 2007, issue of the *Berkeley Daily Planet*, a newspaper published in Berkeley, CA.

The following poems are being reprinted from my book, *Gathering the Grace of Others* (Beatitude Press, Berkeley, 2004): "A Photo of My Parents," "My Mother's Funeral," "Mother and Daughter," "A Semblance of Truth," "The Actor," "The Grandmother," "The Arrival of a Train," "To Stanley McNail," "Picture," "My Father," "Donkey Serenade," "Wettingen, October 1993."

OTHER POETRY COLLECTIONS:

Duo Chapbook—Baroque in the Chaos (Vagrom Press, *Sparrow Magazine*, Fall 1965)

An Octave Higher than Grief (Libra Press, New York, 1970)

Cleft Between Heaven and Earth (Illuminations Press, Berkeley, 1985)

The Galley Sail Review, Vol. XII, No. 2, Issue 40 (Issue 16 of Series 2, Fall 1991)

Gathering the Grace of Others (Beatitude Press, Berkeley, 2004)

TABLE OF CONTENTS

A BANGING

I hear the banging of silverware –
A film crosses my eyes. I see
A mother, my mother, blowing
On a spoon, gently blowing
As if the tides of the sea
Are being uplifted in this breath
Of embrace and release. It is my mother.
My eyes so young, yet seeing all,
She places oatmeal on her wrist;
It is still hot – she blows
The spoon just before my lips.
I do not grasp – it is the trust
Of babies, children, who watch
Their mothers zip and button,
Place hair in place, make pony tails.
It is a trust taking us through
The perils of self-mastery.

What age I was, I cannot tell.
She is there blowing cool air
About the spoon – I had no inkling
Then, that years to come, I will
Have to spoon-feed dignity to her.

LADY WITH MULTIPLE SCLEROSIS

She tells me of the unfathomable
Terror of being an object – the death
Beyond all death, where no one knows
That she too was once fertile, freewheeling,
Bearing two large-boned sons
Who could not forgive her now for being ill,
And by rejecting her, impaled her will to nought.
"I want the minister, the health director,
All the nurses to know I have children,
Though my feet are locked within themselves,
And my hands dance in an idiosyncratic
Beat, I am strong enough to wring your necks
And my mind is stronger than hello –
They don't come – my illness reduces them,
They still want me to carry
The weight of their baggage on their journeys.
I want you to know, I was a mother,
I was penetrated in passion. I moved
Like the best of them – Let them go –
All of you build your house of decay.
I am still all that I am.
I want you to hear that, understand that
I produced two sons healthier than you."

MY MOTHER

When I watch the ballerinas
Spreading their arms like wings
I think of you, dear mother, who loved
The ballerinas and who, up to your death,
Made little pirouettes with your hands
Above your head, the crest and the heart
Of your unfulfilled longing.
I too am moved by that alphabet
Of movement which must be the Russian
Instinct in me – You took me to see Tallchief,
Fonteyn, Farrell – the men I forget,
But my wife said we saw Nureyev.
When I watch the ballet I think of you,
A woman born in a girdle of time
When your mother restricted you –
The stage was dirty, impure, not for
A woman. You were restricted as I, too, was
Banned from even an idea of the ballet.
You made a stage of your presence,
Aped the movements through your life
As we both courted our dreams
And held center stage through the glitter of darkness.

PEOPLE LOOK AT EACH OTHER

Even when they turn away.
They take something for themselves.
The eyes' touch is a prologue of grace and grief.
People look at each other
And then turn away. Murder and love
Are the flickering syllables of touching,
Hiding, preparing, reaching.
We turn and then look again
As if something quite naked, quite
Covered has entertained the landscape.
People look at each other's looking,
Or wait to steal a look, while
The other, head down, undresses,
Deceives, murders or places a paradise,
Back into the touching, the beckoning,
Into the ceremonies, the fluid instances
Of unrehearsed drama –
People look at each other
And then turn away,
This prologue, this rehearsal
Brings the grave, the paradise
Into the separate restlessnesses –
And then perhaps, a smile, a word,
A wink, a seeming preoccupation
With space breaks the boundaries
Of unspoken energy –
People look at each other
Doomed to unrehearsed paradise
And the grace of new grief, new touch.

KEEPING OF THE GUARD

He used to call me Morton
With that Southern drawl
From Alabama – he was
A sergeant but seemed more
Like the extra they asked to complete
Work already done. He wasn't
Really slow nor stupid – in fact,
He may have been bright but floated
In and out of some personal world
Or the orders of the lieutenants and captains
And always when he meets me, he calls
Me Morton – we psychologists were seen
As necessary lunatics – I felt honored
To be called Morton by Ross. But one day,
"Hey doc, I can't shake it, doc. I
can't shake it. I was working the gun
tower – I shot a man in the leg – I
feel so guilty." "Ross, it was your job.
It wasn't homicidal." "Doc, I feel
so guilty – I see that man walk,
with a damaged leg all his life."
"What were you to do?" "Mort, I see
that man all his life, without a leg,
one leg – a damaged body – I'm
so sorry – so sorry."

FORECLOSURE

Things can close up – a valve
May choke on itself, a bladder
May be weary, a love may become
Stale as renewal is impacted.
The lyric is no antidote
To hard-driven fact – "Pay up, buddy."
A fashion of grace
Only masks the forceps
Of exploitation.
So what can we do
When the world is taken
From under our steps,
When sweet-talking crooks
Offer us forever as the real?
What are we to do
When we hurt, others hurt,
When the air we breathe
Can be the sorrow of others,
The dew we feel, the tears of others?
The valve may close up,
The bladder may be weary,
The heart seeks its lyric,
As closing, closing, closing
Is not the way to breathe.

SUSAN IN HAWAII

At this table, we are forbidden
To feed the birds – you remind
Me of this restriction as my right hand
Below the table drops crumbs
And perhaps an entire slice
Of bread to my daily friends. You
Chastise me again as you steal
An onion ring from my plate.
I have not touched the water yet.
You scratch your head, remind
Me that two rums lubricate
My biases which I should
Keep to myself. You steal another
Onion ring, kissing me on the head,
"My hero." At the Hilton, you asked me to see
Another Buddha – perhaps the two hundredth
Of the day. I fell down the stairs
And then arose out of the pyre of helplessness
To walk two more miles by the sea.
You steal another onion ring.
I feed the birds surreptitiously.
I shake my fingers at my Venus:
"No more Buddhas this lifetime."

THE MURDER OF TOOKIE WILLIAMS
Executed by the State of California, 2007

His sister stared at the well-built
Man in the casket. I still heard
His deep voice on KPFA, talking
Intelligently about gangs and his work
With children – the breath of his life
Was now deeply rooted in his mind.
I waited eagerly that night
For a reprieve. I became more angry
And more angry. I did not go
To the vigil that night. I called
The Terminator, speaking to a nice voice,
Saying that as politicians we must
Not evade the critical, the ethical, the moral
Moment. Let us not embrace the executioner
Of life itself – though Tookie was smarter
Than the Terminator, this was not
A question of intelligence – others, like
Mentally retarded invalids, would also
Taste the poison of the State's vengeance.
No, it wasn't exactly a tooth for a tooth,
An eye for an eye. No, Mr. Terminator,
You need another icon, another target,
To refurbish your righteousness –
How else to destroy your own evil,
Your own sinfulness by taking the will
Of the divine and in graceless, primal
Purification you can still live with yourself –
The blemish, the purifier, all in one thoughtless act.

DIALOGUE

"Find yourself a sweet man, a sweet man."
The adagio of a brother's love played on.

"The bills just pile up, the phone, electricity and laundry..."
"Just find yourself a sweet man, a sweet man."

She embraced him by listening to him, but her eyes were tired.
"She wants all the things that she sees on TV and I want to be a
good mother."

"There must be a sweet man for you, a sweet man for you."
I looked at her strikingly primal face, her nose flaring.

But her grief was soft, and her sorrow both dark and sweet.
Her lament linked to something in me, a beast, a terror of
nothingness.

"The rent is up, car repairs, medical bills..."
And she terrorized herself more and more by reciting darkness.

"Just find yourself a sweet man, a sweet man."
I desired her, I made her into a needy profiteer.

My generative self fought with something insidious.
"Just find yourself a sweet man, a sweet man, who will care for you."

At the race track each morning I hear muses mourn,
I hear black men embrace instances of lost photos.

It is not a racial thing I think,
The world is cruelly indifferent to all chapels of dreams.

I desired her and my hands were folded as if in a prayer.
I felt a couplet of sorrow and lechery.

"Find yourself a sweet man, a sweet man," he went on.
And her tears seemed to fall into my folded hands.

THE GRANDMOTHER

She was a grandmother, the stroller
By her side, her white hair, the calendar
Of her experience. She helped the
Child's hand and eyes peek through the fence,
His arms, an eyesight dividing and making an inventory
Of a world he had never seen. Grandmother
Like mother, is filled with first times,
Holding the child safe and yet pushing him
Slightly to risk – the balance of all
Birth and its dangers, never
Quite a failure, always a new spiral,
Straight forward, circular, a birth of worlds:
The many agreements of space.

PHOTO OF MY PARENTS

I look at the marriage
Photo of my mother and father –
The date is most likely 1934
When Europe was in chaos,
And Hitler was employing his toxin of purification.
They looked beautiful. He was tall, slim,
A posture very erect, a dashing example
Of the honest prince. They were in love.
First generation Jews – how life molded
And sculpted them – my father losing
Inches by the years, a pot belly,
A spiteful smile, and she a strength
But with a terrible nagginess. Oh unholy
Grasp of history: to make
A living and carry out dreams. He moved
Other people with his handsome smile. He was bright
And read the *Daily Worker*, books on yoga
And went to the Brooklyn Museum. Oh how
My hearth hurts and laments for the fall
Of a man emptied and seeing me as a competitor
When I did love him dearly. Oh unholy
Mutation of generations, I ache and ache,
A seventy year old man, for the fall
Of my father. I will gift him with as much
Life as I have left: to be both the blessing and the blessed.

LAUNDRY

She picks up each piece as if it is
A life of its own, and perfectly
Folds it – she does this wash
With exactness and preciseness,
With a touch of design I marvel at –
I try – my geometry is called mess.
Hers is not neatness, it is the art
Of perfect reference, the exercise of duty
Somehow perfected in utero,
And consummated in practical grace.

THE PERILS OF DEVOTION
Celebration of Two Men: One to be Married, One to be Ordained as a Rabbi

What calls us can also burden us –
Our deepest loves demand perplexing loyalties –
What seems to make all things lighter
Are closed eyes receiving the warm
Winds of spring, our naive eyes
Opening as if for the first time we see
Birds flutter amid the eyelids
Of flight as our unpossessing hands
Push away the bonds that bind us.

And yet in private, we portray our destinies
Which pain but ennoble us –
We can reinvent each smile, each
Movement, each flutter of the eyes,
Each commandment of a ritual
We are committed to –
What has created us is further created
By us.

Yet, we still must push away those loves,
Close our eyes, receive what is given to us –
And then opening again see tapestries
Of green, rolling hills where the large
Globes of a fawn's eyes,
Alert and captivating, watch us.

What calls us can also burden us
So at times we take a respite
From worldly things and even
        The life of the spirit.
And prepare to live as we prepare
        To leave.

So Michael and Daniel, as you
Arrive at new places,
Where history has both
      Lamented and joyed,
May you possess nothing but be
      Everything,
Be enriched and enriching
As the Creator and created
      Become One.

A POEM FOR PEACE

All armies seem the same—
They strut with the chins of dullards
In a sentimental vise of duty,
A synchronous mating of unripened men
While the elders watch, saluting—
In China, in North Korea, all over the planet
The dead seriousness of patriotic
Stupefication, the vulgar sentiment
To protect family, Country, and some God.

All armies seem the same—the elders
Salute, are proud, know that the ranks
Emptied of anonymous cadavers
Will again be filled by the raw youth
Who vibrate in their chains with images
Of heroism, never imagining the swimming
Of bloody limbs before them.
These are the gifts of mothers and family
A gift returned in metal or casket—
These are the ceremonial rites
That make the deepest evil into virtue.

All armies seem the same to me,
They beat to a metronome of false blessing.
They march to a symphony of blaming.
All armies seem the same to me:
The elders salute, promise is impaled.

SMALL FIRE

All that is good
    And pure
Starts with fire
    And breathes the air
All things fundamental
    Are made of evil and
End with apocalypse.

Come catch me, she says,
    Her hair flowing on a cool
        Berkeley day, truffles,
Coffee and poesie. Her eyes
    Catch my flirtation,
        Giving me a thankful smile,
A reasonable coquette
    Who likes the game
        She plays mildly seriously.
In male parlance, she was cute
    And it was nice
        Being smiled at.

I returned to Proust
    And wondered
Why it all seemed so damn difficult—

Fire of air, puzzling
    Revelation of moments.

MY MOTHER'S FUNERAL

Recollection of you in your casket,
Dark red lipstick, well made-up
For the endless dance, the tango
Of shapelessness and void, you still
Coming to me to ask forgiveness.
You, such a strong force in my life,
Lay still, I placing a book of poems
To lay with you – of course I forgive –
Give thanks for life itself. This surprised
Me, this primal thank you. You had
Your special kind of joy. A veneer
Of conventionalism made life
Safe for you. You were fearful, loving
And shaped me with both forces. You
Moved from me since I always reminded
You of your first love, my father,
Taken early from both of us.
Men adored you, it was your route
Out of immigrant poverty, a celebrity
Of sorts, your peasant mother would
Not permit you to indulge in dance.
I was pleased to hear the many
Who loved you, mourned you. They spoke
Of your class, your stateliness, a distance
And goodness which were our two roads.
You were to come home with us. You
Improved, asked for sausages and eggs,
Waved goodbye to your adoring sister
And then closed your eyes. You had
Become ill, perplexed by your mind's
Primal trickery, the heaviness
In your chest. You did not suffer.
You died peacefully, yet returning,
Asking again and again for forgiveness.

I never thought I would miss you.
The last few years I was your
Darling *bubala*. We both became
Very generous to each other. Still, when
In Florida, I see a Russian profile,
A reddish or silver impeccable hairdo
My body moves forward to greet you again.
We had been afraid of each other. My
Father's presence in me moved you away.
First loves are never forgotten. You did
Share a voice with me that no one else heard.
The poetics of survival, the loyalty
Of co-mingling separateness.

THE ARRIVAL OF A TRAIN

The train coughed, announced
Its territory, the one boy clapping
His hands, jumping in a syncopated
Harmony with this massive dismantling
Of space. His cousin turned white. His
Ears were plugged by his fingers as he turned away.
The other boy jumped even higher than joy,
Running back and forth, observing
His declension from the dream. The train began
To move slowly, the other boy looked up
From a bunker of his fear, releasing
Himself as the train moved away.
The one boy clapped again, raptured
Until space was emptied of the fruition
Of its ecstasy. Two boys, one train,
Tears staining the platform from joy,
Tears staining the platform from overwhelming fear.

THE ACTOR
November 19, 1992

Nonchalance was his gift. Tasks
Slipped from the platter of responsibility
As he waved disaster goodbye,
Greeting us today. He was a brute
With the real world. He disdained
Faults and welcomed its challenges.
Nonchalance was his gift since hugeness
Was his center. He controlled those
Who worked with him through love.
People took his praise and blessed
The challenges of the day. He was
Larger than himself, a politician of the heart,
And we could believe in ourselves, since
He was the great pragmatist – the beautiful liar –
We all loved him – he made us feel good about ourselves.

BARBARO

"We need a hero—
This industry needs a hero,"
Hines, the bright, volatile trainer said in a depressed mood,
As Andrew Beyer steadied himself,
His New York academic mind in the diction of sports bars
But never concealing his philosophical bent.

The undefeated Barbaro, a legend before his next triumph,
Took a wrong step—filled with the dynamics of purpose;
He broke out of the gate early, rambunctious, carrying a world of
dreams—
He was returned to the gate quickly.
I thought nothing would slow this Preakness down, this celebration
of the expected—
Barbaro took a wrong step with a cracked ankle,
He ran further, breaking his leg to pieces.
The jockey superbly contained what was supposed to be released—
The crowd frozen with astonishment, his leg dangling in mid-air,
Tom Durkin, brilliant in his vocal snapshot of two worlds,
Two parallel worlds, one bleeding, the other breathing.

Barbaro now stands in his stall
After surgery.
It is still 50-50—
The surgeon praises his athleticism.
We now promote, celebrate his foals of our dreams:
Brilliant stallion, our slave of greatness.
We finally released you from your pain,
Our pain.

MOTHER AND DAUGHTER

The mother smiled when
I looked at her beautiful daughter,
Not quite fulfilled
As a woman.
The daughter shone
In that wetness
Of light which reveals
To me the shuddering
Of the receptive dark.
The mother smiled proudly,
As if my possessing eye
Gave her something, rather
Than took something away.
It was as if she was
Letting her daughter go
And in that act
Was completing herself.
The mother smiled,
As I could not prevent my looking.
A man had nothing to do with it –
She had prepared nature well.

CAPE COD SCENE

The bush grows from out a bed of sand.
     Its earth is white and berries
     Are upon its leaves. The shoulders
Of the land move in circles of horizon
     And I watch gulls lean their beings
     Into the wind and move over waters
        I taste with sight.
I see ships move in snail-pace dignity
     And I watch two children dressed in red
        Run and flop in the sands.
I walk – I wish to fly and run.
     Sand is on my lips;
        I cannot sing.

THE OTHER SIDE OF PEACE

Again a bird releases me
From the pragmatics of pain.
I hate cars. I watch it hop from fender to fender
Into a pool of clarion light.
It is becoming grand. Steel dissolves
As I watch its marvelous
Meticulous syncopations
Make a new world. I will
Play with it a bit. I dance
With the new world in the fingertips
Of my eyes. It seems happy,
If birds can know glee.
I watch, I move with it into
A pool of a mélange of light.
He is having a harvest of a time.
My stomach then heaves. Human vomit
Displays the entrails of half-eaten food.
I walk away as if carrying death.
I am being soldered to decaying light.
An ancient familiarity has run amok.

SPIRIT

She is the leaf
   That refreshes me
And the root
   That binds me
She is flora and anima
   The dual realms
Of source and deed.
   She reminds and fulfills me.

MEETING A ONCE VIGOROUS FRIEND

He speaks of a slow death.
The leukemia is a slow one,
As he prepares to bet
Belmont at Golden Gate.
A handsome, kind man,
He looks sick as the vibrancy
Of his health has been
Taken from him. His pallor
Invites nothingness. He walks
With a bit of a limp. He is eighty-one.
He asks my age. We are cordial.
He had read my poems
On a small FM station in Marin.
"I have the slow kind." I like this man,
I bless him – another loss – a deep breath
As we try to bait the racing gods
For a winner. It is not a winner we want
Or need. It is a blessing. Time harvests,
Time takes away. We bet as if
We live forever.

SHADOW

He is bound to his chair
Like a Prometheus to a rock;
Each movement, as it is minor,
Still moves him in a major way.
I know him for thirty years –
He was an artist, a drug taker –
He hardly speaks, he grunts,
But understands much as he
Sells his homemade postcards.
We are related by mockery –
I speak a fabricated
Foreign language to him,
Tease him by asking
Whether he or I am crazy –
I torment him endlessly
With babble, fake vocabulary –
He utters his sarcasms
And says enough, enough, enough.
Each day it is the same –
He is glad to see me,
I open the door for him.
When he enters the cafe,
I call him tiger, as he
Moves towards his ritual
Seat, splashing chairs about.
I am deeply embalmed in him –
What in me tears him apart
As stoically he braves my shadow,
His shadow has been lost in me –
Yet bound to the chair,
He arrives each day. I insult
Him each day – enough, he says –
In a way he asks for more.
We are in love; the shadow of mockery
Resurrects each within each.

CARNIVAL IN OAXACA
December 17

It was a carnival, a shuffle of tents
A grammar of space that spelled "thrill."
Roller coaster, concentricities spinning
About one's gut and the molecular roads
Where no meter or avenue marks your end.
It was pepsi cola and dark Indians
Huddling proudly in their serapes
Watching not participating in the shooting
Of ersatz ducks, and the making of light,
Or in the chance and doom in their bingo
Called "lotteria," my daughter playing three games
Her face pale without victory, flushed
In the vibrancy about her, breast-fed children,
Epitomes of all children I have seen,
Barefoot, red-apple cheeks, hair well-braided,
Curious about me and not spiteful nor conceptual.
I bought a Pan de la Muerte and ate it.
He smiled when I ate it after his palms
Gently received my peso. Was it for the home
Or the graveyard? I do not know.
The merry-go-round. All children love the rounds,
The rounds of singing and spinning,
The mysteries of motion going nowhere
And everywhere at the same time.
These dark Indians, white hats and sandals,
Smiling secretly, speaking their own language,
I think of the hills where they live
And of their ancestors in Mitla and Monte Alban,
A syntax I readily felt but did not learn:
The mechanical ducks fall, the lovers kiss,
My daughter and wife walk on each side of me,
And I see that a tourist guide is like a promise
One makes to the farthest mountain of himself.

DUO ON A CAMION

In a crotch of doom
I hear them sing,
A duet and a brotherhood,
One is blind, the other
Compassionate, a crutch.
They first ask permission
From the rough-bearded driver
Who sifts centavos in his hands.
They sing a cancione of love. One's eyes
Are closed, tighter than a clam's shell.
The other's hands seek a harmonic
To orchestrate their strengths. It is lovely:
This warmth obliterates my familiar
January snows, and I hum with their consonance,
Rolling with a movement, huddling a sadness
That is both simple and monumental.
The blind man leans on his friend, who leans
On a pole. It is finished. Palms come down
To me, and I see pesos drop upon
The fleshy banks of a hand. They leave. Gracias.
I hear echoes of a love song I do not know
The name of. Where am I going, coming from?
I see them wait for another bus, and wish
I had another pair of eyes to give as my
Life has been given to me. Gracias.

A WALK

Like a slain lover
He lay in a pool
Of Life's disasters,
His blanket crossed
In cravats of chaos,
The cot of cement,
The former madhouse,
The awaiting cell
For X the murderer,
The slab for Y the murdered.

He lay like a slain lover,
Why, I don't know.
Something about his twisting,
His mouth, agape in wordless wounds,
Yet his contortion was alarming,
So his own flesh and bones
Could be a mattress of comfort.

My wife gave him her tea,
I bellowed about the CEO's,
The bloodied lambs who could not compete,
The interest holders, the tribal
Congress who ache in their
Excessive stomachs.
He gave my wife a thanks
Which pained me more, taking
The cup like a thirsty child,
And my wife delivered the cup to his mouth,
Protecting him from burning himself.
I saw flowers offered to a coffin.
I became quiet, knowing that a
Lover without a love is love withheld.
O Eden, your aimless fall
From wholeness.

TWO YOUNG LOVERS ACROSS FROM ME

Her blonde, silken hair,
Black knitted blouse;
He feeding her a spoon
Of ice-cream, a cup
Below the spoon, to catch
Errant ways. Her
Legs open comfortably,
The dungarees riding lightly
Upon the cornerstone of her pelvis,
Absolutely open, unrestrained
Her hands playing with the coffee cup
Before him, moving her forearms
Forward, touching, not touching,
He touching her hair, cascades
Of blonde silken hair, of skin,
Transfixing the observer.
He reddens, composite
Of shyness and desire, he touches
Her brow, undaunted by expectation.
There is a springtime all about her –
She opens in the field of lilacs, goldenrod,
With birds, gazelles and dancing elephants –
She turns her head away,
Places her thumb between her lips;
He offers another spoonful of ice-cream,
She licks the spoon clean, they hold
Each by the forearms, rocking back and forth.
Then another touch, he leans
Backwards, as a bent willow,
Springs back, touches her cheeks,
Her lips suck his knuckles,
There seems to be a redness
Bleeding from their cheeks –
She takes the spoon, returns it to him –
There is nothing posed,

Nothing even imagined –

It is a dance choreographed
By ancient harvests years ago.
I watch the touch,
Sucking the grace
Of liveliness – they do all from me,
Ah, forlorn, forlorn, forlorn.

BY A POOL
Sfat, 1986

All domestics seem equally unhappy to me.
I sit on the patio of the Rimon Inn
In Israel's sacred city, high upon a mountain.
Susan swims, I sip water to deter dehydration.
My pipe smokes very good. Two women
Walk slowly, I've seen them in Reno,
In Puerto Vallarta, with a broom and basket.
One is exceptionally pretty. Are they Arabs or Israeli?
The hotel charges one hundred a night to sleep.
That would be too much pressure for me
To have a good night's sleep. We are staying
At a hotel for eleven dollars. It is not the money.
My mate and I invent infinite ways
To rediscover our youth – there are ten empty beds
In our room.

All domestics seem equally unhappy to me.
I have seen them in Tahoe, in Acapulco,
I always instantly dream of making love to one
As if their need produces no morality or
My role of "wealth" exempts me from virtue.
I fear that all men who carry wallets are plunderers.
Sfat is surrounded by deep valleys. I have
The impulse to dive into them. I have tamed
My fear of heights, but not my flirtation
With abandonment. I have done well.
The fear remains only as a bitter herb
Or as a reminder of self-hate in childhood.
An only child, I did envy their love of each other.

But that is ancient history. My artifacts
Are lined with a guilt, not that of the Hebrew
But that of the murderer in the dawn of history.
The jealous boy wanting what has power over him,

Learning to be good, so the world redeems him.
I touch the palm tree. Awe replaces possessiveness.
I remember childhood being a crime, without
Cause. It was in the nature of things, the wonderment,
The imitation, the dreams of annihilation.
All domestics seem equally unhappy to me.
The better our parents, the deeper the guilt.
We all kill each other. Jealousy is a powerful love.

THE DOOM OF HOPE

I ride a bus from an exquisite race track
And hear a man whose mouth is hollow
With gum, whose heart is bitter with anger,
Expostulate a loser's ethic, the crooked
Jockeys and the impending annihilation
Of the track when the crowd can take no more.
He wanted to make a day's pay
And he brought home a day's pain.
I hear him, mouth devoid of marrow,
The program held close to his decaying vision,
Convince me of the winner of the next race
Being now run, while his labyrinth of guilt
And enslavery gives a wisdom for all but himself.
"Stay away, they take but do not give."
As he wrestled in his pocket for Gilardi's winners,
July 9, August 10, all but the one for today,
Lost in the crevice of his wallet, where once
His pride lay. The man sleeps now.
I'll look tonight in the paper for the next winner,
Half in jest, half with a gaping mouth.

AN EVENT IN A CAFE

As I dictated a report, a gruff
Poly-transcendental man
Said to me: "You're not
A psychiatrist, are you?"
I said, "Psychologist,"
And he lectured me
About the imperfections of the field:
"More written about a subject
We know nothing about!"
I caressed his aggression;
"Well, we are special animals,
Aren't we?" I got his goat –
The word "animal" choked him
With a personal nausea.
I pondered – was this my murderer,
Is this the moment of my death?
His sword, drawn from his mouth:
"What about the spiritual plane."
He huffed, puffed, chastening
Me with grotesqueries of extermination.
He left – I did point out
That he didn't introduce himself
And knew nothing about me.
"The spiritual" his exit echoed.
Obviously, I said to myself.

INTERCOASTAL

Like a beneficent bonfire,
The sun sneaks
Beneath the clouds,
Delivering itself to ourselves,
As we sit on a bench
On the intercoastal, the companion
Darkness coming to us
Like frescoes parting and becoming,
Until unity dissolves fragments
And my imagination is stilled for a while.

MY VISION

He sees floaters;
This has now been defined as an ailment.
Before, he thought
His glasses were dirty.
Now his careless self
Has been given optic identity.
He feared going blind
And immediately planned

Who would read the Racing Form
To him. God help his wife.
That would be worse than
A leaning tower of a husband.

She always tolerated his not seeing;
"A little boy folly," she sighed.
So near-sightedness does something
To the vitreous: A common wear and tear.

"Make sure no one hits you in the head,"
The experienced opthalmologist counseled.
It was pairs that went to the ark,
And we are given pairs to work together.

He blinks. One can outlast the other.
He cleans his glasses;
Nature has given him unimagined flaws
He diligently had worked for.

IRAQ WAR

I feel betrayed.
The planet has moved from me.
I resolved the murderer in me;
I didn't understand, I left it, him, with them.
It is a serious abandonment –
I feel disowned.
Yet I am doing the rejecting
Who are these men, all over the world
Selling the destructive prosthetics
Of arm, limb and fantasy –
The arm that can immobilize a town,
The foot that can trample the laborer,
The fantasy which makes us a crazed God.

I am among dying friends now –
A burial of promise is the deepest grief.
Who are these people who have
Been selling products of annihilation,
Murder, self-aggrandizement?

I feel betrayed –
The world is filled with criminals,
More than I had thought,
Rich enough to buy classic thoroughbreds
And women my hedonist eye cherishes.
This is a sad time:
Evil is again paraded in ideology.
Who are these men who extend
The beautiful human body
Into the remote control of unending ruin?
I feel betrayed.
I am sick, I have lost humanity,
What am I! Who am I!
Friend, cry on my shoulder,
So I know I am real.

HUMMINGBIRD

It shivers
    A signature
Of proud aloneness –
I watch a cat
Arise from the suspiciousness
of its balance,
Stalk the air with death-like paw,
Stalk it again as the bird moves higher,
    Just an incremental life-saver
    An inch the birthstone of life –
The cat gives up. The hummingbird
    In tremulous equipoise stays proud.
I am the bird and the cat –
    Too proud to spin upon land,
    Too mean to leave well enough alone.

WALKING BEHIND HER

Watching her
Watching herself in every mirror –
This mannequin-groomed beauty
Turns to me – "May I take
A picture of you?"
Flattered, I walked ahead
As she directed, "Turn," and then
"Click" – I was to be in her senior
Photography class. I watched her,
A maroon landscape of lipstick
And matching slacks, impeccably
Set hair, and buttocks
Which excited me – "You will be
In a poem of mine, too." She smiled.
"Every woman I follow looks
Into every window they pass."
She was taken aback. I shouted,
"It is not a criticism – we all do."
She smiled – her echo of confirmation
Not quite heard. I walked past
A shop window – all women look –
Men take a peep, affirming
Not beauty but wholeness – I still walk on.

COMFORTING

Her head lay on his shoulder
As they waited for the light to turn.
Her shoulders held her grief
As they crossed their arms.
In this way the body becomes a soul.
This was comfort – the surrender
To one who is there for our distress.
And then as the light turns green,
Her head rises in a ceremony of alertness.
They cross the street, holding hands.
I am comforted the way we comfort each other.

I HANDCUFF MYSELF

With immense passions –
I yearn for gross self-confirmations
With a winner of a three-hundred-yard drive
And lasso each plastic 40-24-36
Into the testosterone bevy of my culture.
I score more goals on a left wing than Bobby Hull,
And slash the fairways better than Palmer –
I have knocked out the forbidden stranger
With one short right to the jaw
I am embalmed with the great lusts
And possessive goals –
But all I want to have again
Is a hummingbird playing on my eyelids.

EYE CONDITION

My eyes are like two ripe
Apricots ready to drop,
Two fruits of being
I have carried with me
Since the first sight and sense
Of the crib, the caress
And the expanse of the world.

My eyes have been the instrument
Of my lechery, the tools
Of seeing, the harmony
In things, of possessing
And letting go,
Of comforting
And seeking comfort.

My eyes have been two orbits
Dancing about and within,
A universe breathing through me
As I have breathed through them;
They have sensed delight,
Known danger, given a reprieve
To my other lazy senses.

My eyes have been the center
Of the world, the staircase
To all that is in and out,
To everything up and down,
Topsy and turvy. They have
Delivered bewilderment to the self
And drenched the body in the beautiful.

PARIS

The people weave about,
Are still, murmur in cafes,
Look at each other, a good hearted
Labyrinth where some are in a trance
Holding a tourist guide like a bible.
Pigeons and sparrows are all over;
They feast upon the leftovers left by
Ancient carnivores who practice civility.
History stares at me in a daunting
Lullaby: "What do you have to offer me?"
It all seems to work. Nests of community
Are all about – in indifference and touch.
To cross each bridge is to behold
A gateway to some heaven – untouchable
Yet vital in providing auras to our dream.
The birds, the cameras, the churches,
Timeless tapestry of many pasts.
I reach out, step outward: I and it
Become a palpable mystery.

SAMMY THE COOK

Sammy, my friend, the cook
Cooking up a storm – fat
Spins and spills about the functional
Cauldron – stains his hospital
White, and he greets me with shaky teeth
And pale skin. He looks sixty –
Other times, he is the forty-year-old kid
Speaking eloquently on politics
And the dynasties of Chinese history.
There is one thing wrong –
Sammy is on a losing streak –
I can verify this since the horse
He gives me has little chance, as his
Dreams sizzle in the murky kitchen air.
He thinks I am doing well – I am not,
Since whatever winnings I have
Is a passport to the next race –
Sammy is doing worse than I
Since he is abstaining, knowing
He cannot handle the myriad
Of races before him – I am more stubborn
But bleed more. This month he thinks
I am doing well – he cooks and cooks,
Manages his money well in his head.
I am to place a bet for Sammy;
I am part of his dream, doing well,
A pocketful of money, vanishing again,
Again the same dreams Sammy cooks upon.

ON AMTRAK

Watching an obese woman
Eating potato chips –
As she peeked into the bottom
Of a bag, hoping it was bottomless
As her hunger, I held
Her under a microscope
Of non-judgment, as she toasted
The air with the arc
Of a graceful gulp,
A repetitious and methodical
Drop, meticulous, unhurried,
Each declension savored savagely.

She looked at her indifferent mate
Who placed a safety lock
With his finger on the bag;
She then turned on her CD,
Dreaming into the air, as I heard
A minuscule racket sift
Through her earplugs. I sip my soda.
I am hungry, yearn for a meal
At my daughter's father-in-law's
Memorial service.

I marvel at hunger, the mother
In us which feeds ourselves –
The mother in us which wards
Off death with small comforts
And indulgent passions.
I like the way she feeds herself –
It is a passion, limitless but devout.

PICTURE

She stares into the mirror.
A gray hair becomes her metaphysic.
Her lips have become chapped.
She had eschewed lipstick.
She had been a "natural beauty."
She examines her body as no doctor could;
The firmness of youth has not endured.
She is holding court with small losses.
Her bustline excites but only she knows
The blue river of vein, scarring the gift.
She does not feel older, only unhappier.
Why, she does not know. All seemed so whole,
Her family picture in perfect kodachrome.

ADOLESCENT

My daughter examines her face
And makes an ugly grimace.
Her pimples stand like monuments
To an unfulfilled future
And a flawed present. I support
Her inner being, the translucence
Of a smile over all deformity
And what feels to be such.
I cannot persuade her to feel
Differently – I can give her faith –
A faith that her bones and surfaces
Follow an architecture wholly
Perfect and subject only to our care.
She combs her hair and is glad
She is not a plastic blond.
Her boyfriend is pleased with her natural.
This pleases me – she does like herself better.
My daughter examines her surfaces,
Making ugly grimaces until she sighs
A pleasing breath – the discovery
Of much that was well all along.

LIFE-GAZER

She waited on her perch,
A bird of prey, though preyed upon.
She was bait for life's mysteries
Although she cast out its light.
I knew she looked into my rooms
With eyes no smaller than key-holes.
When not looking, she would sweep
Dust and leaves, dirt and feathers
Upon an ancient duster beneath her rocker.
She waited and she gazed and she slept.
What dream-worlds fathomed her being I cannot know,
Nor the hawk which hid in the chemistry of her Illusions:
When I stopped looking, the key-hole went dark.

ODYSSEY

There is a preludium to the spring:
It follows us in a presence of hope.
Some call it childhood, others paradise.
It will be lost, and we follow it
Through echoes and substances of this world.
They say women wait for the man
As he voyages across oceans to find
Continents which are himself. Men
Needed a resting place because they knew
Conquering worlds only leads to tired selves.

So we began twenty-seven years ago,
You, in love with Joyce and Molly Bloom,
And today in giggles and maturity
Living your dream. The prelude, the last echoes
Have all been worthwhile. You, Ulysses
And Penelope have voyaged and waited.
Our marriage is a season none can take
From us – fellow voyager, let us continue
To weave our strands into this magic.

GERALD EDELSTEIN, MD

Dear Healer,
Who taught me trials and tricks of mind,
The fingers of hypnosis which touched
The dying miracle in me, your logical
Rationality not letting me get away
With anything – but you did bless
The frailties which were me,
As if each was an untutored son
Of yours – I learned you passed
Away at the time Bach's Magnificat
Mass recreated my room – I
Cried, I became angry. "He was
A wonderful man," the secretary
Said – a brain tumor. I could
Not fathom that marvelous brain
Being punished by an unfeeling destiny.
Gerry, you wanted me to call you
By your first name – I refused,
My formalism was praise of your
Skills, the child in me refusing to be equal.
I am angry, I shudder, that the marvelous
Brain of yours was a bedlam of chaos.
"Life is only lent to us," the rabbi says.
Death is the finalizer – the good,
The bad, the real, the unreal, the timid,
The boisterous –

Gerry, my gratitude is your rebirth.

AESTHETIC

A parasol of flowers
Revealed her – a parasol
Of flowers concealed her.
This style was the grace
Of a distant seduction –
Come close, I asked her –
She offered me a flower
And I took her stocking,
She offered me a stem
And I tasted her blouse.
What is it you want me to show,
She asked me. I looked
At the lips, a landscape of blossoms.
I smiled a leaf of bewilderment.
Offering me that garden: I wanted
What could not be had.

PORTRAIT OF SELF

We make portraits
      Of each other from pigments –
Your own cross-purposes,
      Color the features of others
With the blacks and reds
      Of our defeats and rage,
Pronounce a frown upon their lips
      When our own mistrust
Disarms us, construct a history
      Of he, they and you, from
Syllables of night where our own
      Journeys are rootless turns.
And once in a while, when our doubt,
      Our topsy-turvy canvas of void
Dissolves in an instant of clarity
      We see a picture, a truth,
Fresher than a new pigment, clearer
      Than any tale or judgment
It is as if we kiss for the first time
      And are present at a new birth.

TO MY DAUGHTER ON CHRISTMAS

I celebrate a gift,
A gift more important
Than the exchanges between men
And those bought in the store
Or made by the labors of hand.
I celebrate a gift
Which unfolds in pain
And in grief, and in emptiness.
I celebrate a gift
Which sings, joys and hates
And lifts me from my shield
Of arrogant adulthood.
I celebrate a gift
Who makes me angry
Who makes me cry
Who makes me doubt
And gives me pride.
I celebrate a gift
Which I cannot possess,
Cannot own or exchange,
I celebrate my daughter
Who, I pray, will allow herself
The gift of her selfhood.

A COUPLE

I see an old couple, a copy of themselves,
Trail each other, the woman
With veined white legs
Pedaling upon tennis shoes,
The man hunched but still over six feet,
His huge Bermuda shorts
Snuggled over his plateau,
A Hawaiian array touching his knees.
She scolds, "Hurry," and he
Shuffles just behind her,
An unlit cigar in one hand,
A towel over the tray of the other –
The more I look, the older they appear,
Yet their short-stepped movements
Are of life's elan – she turns again
But does not scold – her speed has little
To do with him – she is chasing time.
Soon he shall sit down in the lounge chair,
Light his cigar and, before supper comes,
While he swirls the dream smoke about,
He shall scold, "Dress more quickly, dear."

THE LILACS OF YEARNING

Hand in hand, we enter
A garden where a bouquet
Of ghosts lingers on our fingers –
They seem to cut, they seem
To become an atmosphere
All around us –
We search about, become
Tentacles of need – we are pulled
Apart. Boughs of
A promised bracelet of bloom
Capture us – an aroma
Permeates the air – the insubstantial
And the real reinvent our sense –
It is the lilacs of yearning
Where everything sensate
And promised grips us
With the inventions
Of a quivering paradise,
Where ghosts and promise
Stay still and then lead.

JACK'S ASHES

When I see the ashes
Of those who tickled
Me with joy and confusion,
Rivals and partners –
When the architecture
Of life is the ashes of grief,
And I see those ashes
Dispersed about the wind,
About the roots of trees,
The beds of roses and lilacs,
I cringe in a faulted nobility
And surrender begrudgingly,
To a nasty miracle –
I become the miracle of the rose,
The stillness, the stillness
Of a scream, in the lyrical grace
Of hysterical bewilderment
At the passing of all.

THE DOVE

This beating machine,
      Symbol and process,
           Chalk-eternity

Of a million hopes,
      An egg-like swelling
Pulsing on a prideful
      Indifference and sweet
Enchantment of what is flight
      And what is attainment.

Mirror of tranquility, the world
      Rains blood upon you,
Invoking your calm at the very
      Moments of its disaster.

CANNED FOODS – NOVEMBER, 1992

Little children sit in nests –
The mothers, mostly black,
Wheel them about –
Some men throw shaving lotion,
Blades and tv dinners
Of turkey and beef stew
Into the carts – the kids at times
Link their fingers and a brother
Or sister pushes the cart,
As if each sibling was
A miniature pope, blessing
The air with random celebration
Of "Me too," "I want," and just plain "Aaa."
It is nice here. There are no loud noises,
And the tastes are simple, the children pleasant.
I buy a Baby Ruth and walk the aisles.
A child pinches my pants, and I pinch
His cheeks, while others play hide and seek
Or rebuke the stranger, looking with one
Open, dark eye, from a sanctuary of mother.
I look for cheap batteries, unknown brands,
Move my saliva about, in pangs of interest.
Tomorrow we vote – I'd like to tell
Mr. Bush and Mr. Clinton that their limousines
Do not fit these children, nor my doomed promise.

STUBBORNNESS

My mother is in love with
Persona – no doubt she is
Called the prettiest
80-year-old woman alive.
She is impeccably dressed
And my wife resents the money
She spends on herself – she sees
It as being taken from me –
Somehow, I do not see the beauty,
I see the stubbornness –
Somehow, I do not see clothes
But the protection from blemish –
The love affairs, which were
Totally forbidden –
So my mother annoys me,
But I don't totally
Deny her, her stage.
She fights death
Like a star,
And only I know
Her secret mourning
Which sexed me
Into a poet
And made us
Life-long lovers.

RACE TRACK

They ask each other
If the other had "it."
Trying to be assured
That a double defeat
Makes a single success.
Each approaches the other,
Then moves away
As if the other bore the prize –
Was thus responsible
For the loss.

These dumb nags control
Men playing out primal games,
Dictate who wins,
Who loses, who possesses
The ultimate female –
Who is favored, throne-like,
As the thoroughbred flesh
Blindly, athletically
Circle their destiny,
Men cheering, despairing –
Who is favored, who is doomed.

MY FATHER

You cursed me from your death bed
As you condemned yourself for failing me.

Your vanity could not be used for survival,
Your temper unable to move the world again.

You protected me from pain, yet made me a thief
Of your opportunity, trampled actor,

Handsome man, you took the real too personally,
Mistaking its scorn as a rejecting lover.

ON A CORNER OF VAN NESS

Years have passed – she like
Everyone has aged, but not her teddy bear.
Close to the opera house,
She sits on the curb, her large teddy bear
Held across her legs – I carry
Verdi, Puccini with me, nodding
To her who nurtured and is nurtured by the doll.
I nod to her – she asks for nothing
And is unencumbered by the real.
I am hungry – she will not come to dinner
With me – she is absorbed by her
Child, who also asks for nothing.
I am happy to see that she endures.
O holy planet, what heart has she become
To give a love she had never received.

THE ASH

Floats before me, a leaf-like
Atom, simultaneous
Breath of Fall, after
My fall (body failing itself).
Where did it come from,
Uprooted with a past,
Now without a center,
It turns about like a swooping
Butterfly absorbed in beauty.
An ash turning,
Floating, stopping a second
Before me. I do not know
Your history, your roots—
You are everything
And nothing to me.

THE EYES

They reach into me, turn
My gut around or presume
An understanding when nothing is said.
The language of a stare is a wall
Or a battering ram, to tell
Me to mind my own business—or a hate
I do not understand. My mother's
Eyes always looked me over, the topsy turvy
Terrain of my messiness.
My wife pleads with her eyes, as she
Also celebrates some holiness she is
Practicing. I stand a friend to attention
With the missile of my eyeballs,
With perhaps a slight lift of the eyebrows.
"I'm no one to monkey around with,"
These say, and I may even roll my eyes;
"There's no saying how crazy I can be."
The look is the caress and touch of the will,
The blossoming, the seduction, the conquest.
We look into but also become unto.
Our eyes are walls, wells and also thralls
Where we devour, digest and become the world.
Sorrow's vocabulary is in the eyes
Despite the words of hope and pleasure.
I look into his eyes and see, feel,
A hardship of history, the tumult of pain.
His adult solves problems, but his child weeps
        Perpetually.
The head may bend, but the eyes
Tell us of shame, tell us whether
The shame is sweet or distasteful,
Tells us about the hidden pride,
The toxic guilt.
So when you look at me, be careful your eyes
Do not become my heart, and my heart your eyes.

BENEFACTORS OF THE ANIMAL

Her back glistened, the sweat
Of a youth on the prowl
For her second self,
Defined by instinct. Her eyes
Followed her well-sculpted
Adonis to wherever he went,
Bending this way and that, tortured
With restraint as the cream of her yearning
Lay on the tip of her tongue, licked
His ears with syllables of
Heaving desire. She looked
Him over, from toe to head,
And then played with a fork,
In and out of his mouth, teasing
And satisfying him with food.
Shapely, blond, an icon of fantasy
Which passed through my mournful
Self, she gave me a smile—
I, who had dreamt of death that night
As the tradewinds pummeled the house,
Felt my self redeeming itself, not
Exactly through lust, but in a harmony
Where nature prepares our generative self
To kiss and open as only an animal can.
I am left with a loss which achieves
A graceful awe, and a loss of self,
A dual tongue: one of desire
And one of lost desire.

THE DEBT – MY FATHER

He was at the mirror,
His skin sallow,
Reflecting a heartless
Despair, a quiet panic.
He was going to the union
Meeting—the union
Was the male nurse,
Caring for and hearing
Anger and disappointment.
It was where abuse was cleansed
And yet promise defeated,
Outrageous savagery.
He would give it to them—
I look at his looking of himself,
His dimples, once adorable,
Were hollow harbingers
Of dying. I knew it.
I wanted so much to say, "I love you,
Take good care of yourself."
But nothing came from my throat.
Was it my place? Or was
He another hero, alone on
His ageless "my own two feet."
My love, my fear was petrified
In a disquieting silence.

A TRYST WITH NON-BEING

Little did I know that evening,
When the light was absorbed by the dark,

When at twelve or thirteen I walked
To the hotel to peek at entertainment,

A ventriloquist, a puppet show,
Or some display of song and dance—

Little did I know I would see my father
Lay in the casket, his troubled mind at peace,

See my mother, the queen of fashion also lay
At rest as I put a book of my poems,
An Octave Higher than Grief, on her still chest.

Little did I know that the price
We pay for loving is deepest loss,

Little did I know that I would pain
To any of my wife's, in our rehearsals

For absolute farewells—

Little did I know that evening,
When the night light was absorbed by the dark,

That I would shake in terror
When I partnered the moon's respite.

THE HEART

The heart is something
Like a bird—perpetually beating,
Fanning of wings, something
Akin to the soft rapid
Kiss on each cheek
By a mother.

At rest, it is a breathing
Embryo, which swells
And relaxes in the airspring
Of our body.

O small cathedral,
Abode, animal,
Mystic matter,
You seek not just food,
But that music,
That tissue, resonance
Which tenderly subdues,
That lightness which expands
Will, that caring
Which breeds power
To be in the world, to make
Monuments which make
Us bigger than we are—
But always room for that abode,
O small animal,
Mystic matter,
Ceaseless pulse.

IN PRAISE OF THE DEVOTED

He strides to *shul*, my bearded
Friend by a distant admiration,
He walks with both a buoyant élan
And a profound spirit of darkness

As he again seeks renewal in repetition.

He seems to carry God within him
As his brisk walk takes him
Again and again where his God
Is a perpetual atmosphere of tribal memory.

His spine straight, his head held high,
I imagine the oneness of the congregation—
With one voice and then the multiplicity
In the silent prayer—each *davening* alone.

(A same history in a personal way)

He walks with a vitality, a spirit
Of rootedness—of mission—the goal
No doubt re-birth through repetition,
The defiance of death through devotion.

I sit and watch him disappear—
An artery of faith connecting me to him—
Pray for me, pray for me, yes, pray for me,
And I will live for you—live for you.

DEBTS

Debts are two kinds:
The kind we really can control
And those which control us.
The first relates to our hunger,
The latter, to the wishes of our parents.

A SEEMINGLY TOUGH MAN

He held the puppy close to his chest,
Brined, weather-beaten by a career
      Of seasons.
His undisciplined beard, black
Hat and coat struck me as
      A full-term mourning
In a half-full life.

He walked by the window, where I
      Sit and court the world,
      A world made of the real
And my making of it. I see
      The halcyons of sea and shore
      And the past he came from.
He seemed dazed, enraptured
In his carrying another heartbeat
      Close to his heart.

I felt a lapse in my hunger
As I watched him nuzzle
      His face upon the puppy's belly,
This large man, a life being fulfilled
By this mutual benevolence.

INTRUSIVE MERCY

Something cannot be killed in us.
I study amethysts, opals, the rings of ladies,
The stones of Jerusalem,
The glass of Saint Chapelle.

Something cannot be killed in us.
I watch the business avenue of Saint Michel
From the umbrellas to the Sorbonne's eye,
Even the MacDonald's staring at Luxembourg Gardens
Seems very French, as do the pigeons.

I return after twenty-five years.
Something in us cannot be killed.
We can abuse it, discard it,
Live out its memory by grieving,
But the sun, young love and prayer
Endure their own passing—something
In us cannot be killed—will not be killed.

A MOTHER ON THE DEATH OF HER SON IN IRAQ
Oakland Tribune, July 7

"Jan Martinez said she was proud
she found out her son was being
sent to Iraq but feared he might
be injured or killed. But we never
think these things can happen to us."

It is a toxic pride that kills
And undoes the womb—
A pride of a mother
Bragging about the son
Who will do the killing
For the neighborhood of thoughtless
Ideologues—she has a brave
Son, a good son, but "I never
Thought it could happen to us."
Many male bodies are lain
To rot before they become
The fathers they moved towards—
These mothers pamper
Their sons with a patriotic mediocrity—
I am proud of my son, I will
Bury him with many medals—
No other woman will have him.
Not even the magic of grandchildren
Dilutes the toxin of a genderless invention.

MY FATHER

My father always placed
His keys and money
On one side of the bed
As many do with their dentures.
As a very young tot, I then
Wondered why he did not keep
The artifacts of life
In his trousers.
Each night he hung his always
Pressed and cleaned suit
And shirts upon perfect hangers.
He was said to have had
The best smile in the world.

O dark root of chaos, quagmire
Of self, unsteady on this earth
Despite such order, he did not belong
Here; harder on self
Than on his clothes, he could not find
The order which navigates
Us through the "disorders and sorrows"
Of this lamentable journey.

So I carry his disorder within me,
In part made of love, in part of hate,
His abandonment of himself—
The indifferent, beautiful suits
Still pleading, "Please make me perfect again."

THE MOTHER

My wife finally closes
Her eyes with grandchild
On her bosom—
They are enveloping
Each other.
I feel triumphant—
All strains, contradictions,
Dissolve, as the fluttering
Sobbing child captures bliss.
I hear the soft viola
Attending to all that is good.
I say many times now, "I'm glad
To have lived to be a witness."
I am more appreciative
Than I feel.
May I live so the little one
May learn one good thing from me,
Just one, in an enduring way.

THE RIGHT TIME

I am a seashell
Listening to far echoes
Which seem never to come.
Hours pass, I am the fisherman
And the ship stalled
On the rocks of itself.
Words, thoughts, are banned—
They seem to go inward
Venging the inspired heart
With sterility. I listen
And it is deafening—almost
A dying with no death, a void
Where clutter itself further numbs.
Everything matters, nothing matters.
I am still—stare into myself—
It is a blundering without error,
It is almost a death with no pain
Or a caul—I listen—one must
Be a fool to attend to nothing
For so long—and yet it is I who seem
Attended to by a wand waiting
For its magic. Suddenly Botticelli's,
Venus awakens from a hardened shell,
A portal opens—the flood does come.
But it is shaped by the very numbness
Which had stifled the breath of invention.
Something, someone speaks to me—
I am in a panicky harmony. Everything
Breaks upon and within me and I am
Reinvented, becoming a chaotic peace.

THE INCINERATOR

I would tie the papers,
Stopping a while to review
The comics, look at a pretty person
Or cut out coupons for free baseball cards.
I sat on a stack of papers
Like a happy hobo on a freight car.
Alone in the small cabinet, the black handle to the fires
Coldly before me, I would then
Toss the mounds into the mouth
Where a silent dragon consumed each thing.
And it was a completion and perhaps
A simulated destruction, purging
Something in me. And then one day,
When I can't remember, something
Dangerous occurred. I could not touch
That handle and when I did, I feared
My hand would be caught or that I
Now would be devoured by that animal
Inside the wall. I shivered. I was
In a paralysis of being. The cabinet
Housed demons – to bring out the papers
Was no longer a favor or a treat.
It was to face the X of all things
Unknown. Little boy, what was the danger?
Comfort yourself. To grow is to learn hell.

DONKEY SERENADE

It could be considered a mistake:
Where the horse glides, is impatient, the donkey, with a still step,
Cups his foot down, and its instinct
To go forward is somewhat of a miracle.
Children like donkeys and so they may.
I want the world to stop now.
Thoroughbreds are too quick,
Humans too spiteful. I like the *klutz*.
I am also a stumbler, stumbling
Through Italian trains, sight-seeing
With my agreeable mate. I still
Can carry baggage. This is my souvenir of Europe.
I am still the beast of the family,
The conveyor belt between points of interest,
Laboring through aisles with five pieces
Of special leather in hands and on shoulders.
It did not kill me, while she glided
Past second class to find seats or exits.
Italian women seem to like me, especially
When I spoke French. They, too, liked donkeys.
I fear their short skirts are more protections
Than entrances. But donkeys can wait.
We go on and on and if we stay in one place,
We save ourselves a trip. We never
Make mistakes, for we totally are an error.
Everything goes past us, even our mates.
But sometimes we smile, and chew our food slowly
And even have songs written to us, songs written to us.

SOCIAL ART

She sees herself as a part of art
That is art in public places.
For fifty-one years she brushed
      Crumbs from off my chest,
Wiped chocolate from the sides
      Of my cheeks – she sees
Herself as art in public places.
      I buy her cardigans, I buy
      Her jewelry, I even kiss
Her toes. For fifty-one years, she hands
      Me a toothbrush, presses my pants,
      And in a wink of magic
Takes from the corner of a closet
      A lost beret or a
      Cashmere sweater. She sees
Herself as art in public places.

Who would guess that I make the choice,
      As she models her attire before me?
      When she is pleased, she
Is uplifted – she kisses the cheek
      Where chocolate may still be,
      And pinches my behind,
Reminding me of the important things.

AN EVENING: MEXICO CITY – WINTER 1967

We come in from
A damp city evening
The concrete slippery,
Our backs hard and cold

From sitting too much
In an arena where Russia
Outclassed a team from Chihuahua
Where we saw three games

For the price of a few pesos.
Our daughter's ears itch
Around the tiny holes
Where tomorrow her golden ear-rings

Will be placed. You make
Hot chocolate and I figure
Again the *presupeuesto*
Stating to all Mexicans

In this fashion
I am not a Rich American.
We calculate so our next *casa*
Will have a garden

And how much we shall bring
With us to San Francisco.
I take a California wine
Down to the bar and a corkscrew

Unleashes our savior tastes.
Things warm. A Beethoven concerto
And a book about orchids.
And I dream about plays

Produced on stages,
Stages of my mind and Broadway.
It must still be raining.
I feel warm in the casa of hope.

WETTINGEN – OCTOBER 10, 1993

I walk, passing trees,
Trees coloring and leaves dying
Like New England and I come
Upon a golden bush where
Hundreds of birds, in a choir
Of winged agitation
And immense chatter
Taxi through leaves
Scrambling in and out
And above. It was a magic bush.

Two days later, I, walking
With Susan, seeing a home
Or two of magic, in much green,
The reds of leaves, the orange
Of flowers. "Come see my
Magic bush" and fingers
To fingers my renewed wife
And I walk. There were no more birds.
The bush was quiet like a womb
Must be after delivering, healing,
Preoccupied with its own peace.

I was told they migrated south
That the quilt of wings,
A configured celebration,
Was the beginning of a journey.
I did not make much of my loss
Since other things as home and hills,
Fresh bread remained. I now
Sit, myself ending and beginning,
Chatting and being still. Events in memory
Are choreographed in a flaming dance,
Configured with bush, ashes and treats of life.
I cannot grasp nor penetrate anything.
Everything now flows in and out of me
As if I were a bush, a way-station for the world.

OUR VISITORS NOT QUITE GUESTS

The bird taps on our window
Each morning, an enemy of itself.
It is his reflection which baffles him
And energizes him. He is staking
Out his territory for a nest. Another
Bird clicks, circles our window
Now covered with a white cloth.
I did hear them this morning.
It was very hot. They disappeared,
As I did, this afternoon. Will the nest
Be built, do I have it right?
They are welcome but seem to doubt
Who they are, and where they are.
Click, click, the beak on the window.
Instinct drives for survival becomes topsy turvy.
I'll wait until tomorrow – will I hear
The nip nap on the window? Have we saved
Each from himself, or have we made each
Captive of himself, I don't know.
Click, click, the window is played upon –
Nipping at reflections,
They ignore our crumbs.

TO STANLEY MCNAIL

When we miss someone
We miss a part of our selves –
You left the hospital
Against all advice.

Leaning by the mailbox
You said, "I'll beat this."
Death rattling in my pocket,
In the linings of my clothes,
I did nothing – nothing.
The pugilist in you was
Defeated by a greater power –
I do miss you – you were
Given permission by us to conquer
What was too insidious –
You were a tyrant, a lover
Of men and of the poetic.
You made no bones about it –
Your lechery was mine, what does
It matter the form – the élan was Godly.

I hear your voice from time to time:
"Write a poem a day to keep me alive."

THE HOMELESS

Each night I take my constitutional,
Four or five glyphs of darkness
Ask me for money. Several wheel
Carts into some doorway. I marvel
At the contained steppe where each climb
And walk into both a shield and nest
Of blankets, where only dark ski caps
Move incrementally like birds,
Inching to burst forward, then withdrawing into safety.
A part of me would like to wander, hole up,
As survival is sole expectation, fulfillment.

From out a shade, a corner, my peace
Is shattered. I do not know what to give.
I am angered – my constitutional
Is no longer my grace of abandonment.
Reminders are all about me, of humanness,
Of vultures, of diseases, of helplessness.
All my life interruption meant,
"Think of me and not yourself."
What can we give to make others whole?
I walk – darkness fragments into ghosts
Of itself – this country bares casualties,
Pieces of itself which are hidden in slogans.

TALES

Our faces are narratives
      Of our history,
Our history is the drama
      Of where our desires go –
Our desires, the pulse
      Of our blood.
Our blood is our primal
      Dance.
We wander this garden,
And from all corners of the earth,
The lilacs of yearning blossom
Devotions, as chaos surrenders.

TERRITORY

I wonder what he discovers
In our mutual space –
Leading two collies
Who lead him – he has
Always staggered a bit
Each day I have seen him,
But he straightens his being
Abruptly as if cutting
Through a haze of nothingness.
I wonder those senses
Which take us through
A world, unknown in mode
Or territory – how we manage
Our ailments to stay level.
He speaks to me each day;
The boundaries move about
As intonations change –
He modulates his collies,
I flatter them – he smiles
In gratitude. I wonder
A world without sight – the world
Could be like chess pieces
To move him about – the collies
Ignore me – they stand
In graceful vigilance –
The gatekeepers of his world.

LIVELY SYNCOPATIONS

Fawn – timid ballet slipper –
In the early season of green –

      It leaps darts selfish with form
      Eyes heightened by the newness of it all

      It scampers and almost it seems
      The bush looks out from the eyes

      It is not shyness – it is merely
      The baleful praise – beauty's explosiveness –

Salmon swiftly give blood a form
Following primal calendars

Repeating instinct – sacramental mating
My eyes swim with prehistoric envy –

      Animal to animal, I have lost two feet,
      Gills, the freedom of habit real travel.

      If I could trade my brain –
      I'd be the water – fooled you, salmon.

ABORTED ARGUMENT

"You make more sense when you're silent,"
My mate of thirty-one years says.

I smile. I favor her sarcasms to her criticisms. Her father
admonished her when she
Failed an exam – a 99 instead of 100. (Cruelty resides in perfection
as a snake in grass.)

"You make more sense when you kiss me,"
Freaks of nature we are whole in touching.

Loving and hating the spoken word
We both fear criticisms – (her father and my mother
Were militant hygienists.)

"We better keep both our mouths shut,"
Cheek to cheek we dance and embrace.

Reminding each other that the enemy was
Obedient parents – too loyal to some tribal law.

PRAYER

Lift me up, let me reside
A bit higher than myself, to see
Perspectives without judgment,
To breathe easily without submission.

Cradle me, somewhat above the earth,
But not too high, where both praise
And sadness are not quite in me,
But in the nature of everything surrounding me.

Permit a holy transcendence,
But an earthly connection, where nothing
Threatens and nothing drugs,
Where each thing pays reverence to itself.

Allow me respite without defeat,
A simple seeing, a challenging acceptance,
Where all things are in their place, and all wrong
Is a mere dislocation to be healed by simple caring.

A SEMBLANCE OF TRUTH

Appears – when we stop
And the blue brilliance unfolds
Or rather a hummingbird shivers
In meticulous abandonment
And we are caught in a special awe
Or when the lips of the volcano,
In still-life rage, pierce the momentary –
There is that semblance of truth
When her smile becomes what is called
Radiance and her skin, all of touch,
When the melody distills into an echo
Enclosing us in an envelope of openness.
(So we still seek, top heavy in the wind,
Creating monsters of
This and that, such and such.)
A semblance of truth
Appears in momentary responses, when
Fall takes us as a lover or Spring
Seduces our eyes with chapels of bud.

I may go, may go deeper into darkness
Or find my natural body in a natural way,
But there is nothing that can deter
The absolute stillness of a snowflake
Or the grace of your becoming smile.